Product Design Made Easy

All You Need To Know About Product Design

Peter N. Dan

Copyright

Dedication

To all the product designers out there,
This book is for you.
You are the unsung heroes of the tech
world, tirelessly working to create products
that are intuitive, elegant, and delightful to
use. You sweat the small stuff, obsess over
the details, and never settle for good
enough.
You are the ones who turn ideas into reality,
who transform vague concepts into tangible
experiences. You are the ones who make
our lives better, easier, and more enjoyable.
So this book is dedicated to you, the
designers who make it all possible. Thank
you for your hard work, your creativity, and
your passion for making great products.
May this book inspire you, challenge you,
and help you continue to push the
boundaries of what's possible.
With deepest respect and admiration,

Peter N. Dan.

Table of Content

Introduction

Have you ever looked at a product and thought to yourself, "I could have designed that better?" Maybe it's a clunky kitchen gadget that doesn't quite fit in your drawers or a frustratingly complicated phone charger that always seems to break. We've all been there. But what if I told you that you don't have to settle for mediocre design? Design is everywhere we look, from the products we use every day to the buildings we walk by on our daily commute. But what is design, really? Steve Jobs once said, "Design is not just what it looks like and feels like. Design is how it works." In other words, design is not just about aesthetics, but about functionality and user experience. In this book, we'll explore how to make product design easy and accessible for everyone, regardless of your background or experience. Whether you're an entrepreneur launching a new product or simply a consumer looking for more aesthetically pleasing and functional products, this book is for you.

Over the course of this book, you can expect to learn about the fundamental principles of design, such as user-centered design, the importance of prototyping, and the role of iteration in the design process. We'll also delve into topics such as designing for accessibility and sustainability, as well as the role of technology in product design.

But we won't just be discussing theory - we'll also provide practical tips and exercises to help you apply these principles in your own design projects. By the end of the book, you'll have the tools and knowledge you need to create beautiful, functional products that truly meet the needs of your users.

Before we dive in, let me tell you a story. Once upon a time, a group of engineers were tasked with designing a new airplane cockpit. They went through countless iterations, trying to find the perfect design that would meet all the necessary criteria. After months of work, they finally came up with what they believed was the perfect design.

The only problem? The pilots who tested the cockpit couldn't figure out how to turn on the engines. Despite all the hard work and expertise that went into designing the cockpit, the end result was unusable because it didn't take into account the needs of the users.

This story highlights the importance of user-centered design, which is at the heart of the principles we'll be exploring in this book. So grab a cup of coffee, get comfortable, and let's embark on our journey to making product design easy and enjoyable for everyone.

Chapter 1: Introduction to Product Design

Hey there, fellow design enthusiast! Do you ever find yourself geeking out over cool products like a sleek new phone or a fancy coffee mug? Well, behind every great product is a team of designers who poured their hearts and souls into creating it. Product design is all about making everyday items more enjoyable to use. It's like taking a regular old stapler and turning it into a funky, rainbow-colored unicorn stapler that makes you smile every time you use it. But let's not pretend that product design is always rainbows and unicorns. There are times when the design process can be downright frustrating. Like when the team spent hours trying to figure out why their new toaster wouldn't pop up the toast (spoiler alert: they forgot to put in the springs!). Despite the occasional hiccup, product design is an exciting field that allows you to flex your creative muscles and create something that people will love. In this book, we'll guide you through the process of designing products that not only look great but also function flawlessly. So grab your sketchbook and let's get started!

What is product design?

Product design is the process of creating things that are useful and look good. It's like making a sandwich - you choose the ingredients you want, put them together in a way that works, and then add a little flair to make it look appealing. Product design is about taking an idea and turning it into something that people can use and enjoy. Product design is the process of creating things that people use in their everyday lives, such as phones, furniture, toys, or kitchen appliances. It involves designing products that are both functional and visually appealing, while also considering factors such as user experience, manufacturing feasibility, and sustainability. At its core, product design is about solving problems for people. Designers identify a need or a problem that a particular product can address, and then create a solution that meets those needs in the most effective and efficient way possible. This can involve a range of skills, including sketching, prototyping, and testing, as well as an understanding of materials, manufacturing processes, and user behavior.

Ultimately, product design is all about making people's lives easier and more enjoyable by creating products that are intuitive, efficient, and aesthetically pleasing. It's a fascinating field that combines creativity, engineering, and business savvy, and has the power to shape the way we interact with the world around us.

Why is product design important?

Product design might not seem like the most glamorous or exciting field at first glance, but let me tell you - it's a crucial part of our daily lives. From the coffee mug you drink out of in the morning to the phone you check before bed, almost everything you use has been designed by someone. But why is product design so important? Well, for starters, it's all about creating products that people want to use. Designers are always thinking about how to make products more user-friendly and intuitive, whether it's by improving ergonomics, simplifying interfaces, or adding delightful little details that make a product feel special.

But product design isn't just about aesthetics and usability - it also plays a big role in sustainability. By designing products that are made from eco-friendly materials, can be easily repaired, or are built to last, designers can help reduce waste and minimize our impact on the environment. And let's not forget about the economic benefits of good product design. When a product is well-designed, it's more likely to be successful in the marketplace, which in turn can create jobs, drive innovation, and fuel economic growth.

But perhaps most importantly, product design has the power to inspire and delight us. Think about how it feels to unbox a new gadget or sit in a beautifully designed chair. Good product design can make us feel happy, comfortable, and connected to the world around us.

So the next time you use a product that just feels right, take a moment to appreciate the designers who made it possible. And if you're thinking about going into product design yourself, know that you'll be joining a field that's not only important, but also endlessly fascinating and rewarding.

The process of product design

Ah, the process of product design - a wild and woolly journey filled with creativity, iteration, and a healthy dose of caffeine. If you're interested in designing products, understanding the design process is key. So, let's dive in!

First things first - before any design work can begin, you need to identify a problem or need that your product will address. This can involve researching your target market, identifying pain points or gaps in the current product landscape, and brainstorming potential solutions.

Once you have a general idea of what you want to create, it's time to start sketching. Sketching is where the magic happens, as you turn your ideas into visual concepts that can be refined and iterated upon. This is the stage where you'll want to let your creativity run wild - no idea is too crazy!

From there, you'll move on to prototyping. This is where you'll start to turn your sketches into physical objects, using materials like cardboard, foam, or 3D-printed parts. Prototyping allows you to test out your design ideas and identify any issues or challenges that need to be addressed.

Once you've refined your prototypes and are happy with the design, it's time to start thinking about manufacturing. This can involve creating detailed technical drawings, selecting materials, and working with manufacturers to ensure that your product can be produced at scale.

And of course, no product design process would be complete without testing. You'll want to get your product in front of users and gather feedback on everything from usability to aesthetics. This feedback can then be used to refine your design and make it even better.

Throughout the entire process, communication and collaboration are key. You'll be working closely with other designers, engineers, and stakeholders to bring your product to life, so clear communication and a willingness to listen and collaborate are essential.

In the end, the process of product design is all about taking a concept and turning it into something that people will love and use. It's a challenging, rewarding, and endlessly creative journey, and if you're up for the challenge, it's a career that can offer endless possibilities and opportunities for growth.

Overview of the book

The product design book that I outlined is a comprehensive guide that makes product design easy to learn and understand for beginners. It's divided into several chapters, each of which covers a specific aspect of the product design process.

The book starts with an introduction to product design, defining what it is and why it's important. It also includes lighthearted anecdotes and stories to make the content more engaging and relatable.

From there, the book moves on to topics like research and ideation, sketching and prototyping, design principles and aesthetics, manufacturing and production, and user testing and feedback. Each chapter includes detailed explanations, practical tips, and real-world examples to help readers understand the concepts and apply them to their own projects.

Throughout the book, there is an emphasis on making product design accessible and approachable, without sacrificing depth or nuance. The tone is conversational and engaging, with a healthy dose of humor and personality to keep readers interested.

In addition to the main content, the book includes exercises, activities, and case studies to help readers apply what they've learned and develop their skills. There are also resources and references for further reading and exploration.

Overall, the product design book is designed to be a comprehensive and engaging guide for anyone interested in learning about product design. Whether you're a student, a hobbyist, or a professional designer, this book has something to offer.

Chapter 2: User-Centered Design

User-centered design is like baking a cake for your best friend's birthday. You want to create something that they will absolutely love and enjoy, so you start by asking them what their favorite flavors and ingredients are. You take their preferences into account and come up with a recipe that is tailored to their tastes. The end result is a cake that not only looks beautiful, but also tastes delicious and is exactly what your friend wanted.

In the same way, user-centered design is all about creating products and experiences that are tailored to the needs and preferences of the people who will be using them. It's a design approach that puts the user at the center of the process, prioritizing their needs, desires, and behaviors.

User-centered design involves a deep understanding of the people who will be using the product or experience. This can involve research and analysis of user needs and behaviors, as well as user testing and feedback throughout the design process. By taking a user-centered approach, designers can create products and experiences that are intuitive, enjoyable, and effective.

But user-centered design isn't just about creating products that people like - it's also about creating products that solve real problems and make a positive impact on people's lives. By understanding the needs and challenges of users, designers can create solutions that address real pain points and improve the overall user experience.

At its core, user-centered design is about empathy and understanding. It's about putting yourself in the shoes of your users and designing with their needs and desires in mind. And in the end, it's about creating products and experiences that people love and appreciate - just like a delicious, personalized birthday cake.

Understanding the user

Understanding the user is like going on a first date - you want to get to know them, understand their interests, and figure out what makes them tick. Just like how you wouldn't plan a date without knowing what your potential partner likes, you shouldn't design a product without understanding the needs and desires of your users.

When it comes to product design, understanding the user is a crucial part of the process. It involves research, analysis, and empathy, all with the goal of creating a product that meets the needs and preferences of the people who will be using it.

One way to understand the user is through user research. This can involve surveys, interviews, focus groups, and other methods to gather information about users' needs, pain points, and behaviors. By understanding the user's perspective, designers can create products that are tailored to their needs and preferences.

Another important aspect of understanding the user is empathy. This means putting yourself in the user's shoes and seeing the product from their perspective. It involves considering their emotions, motivations, and goals, and designing with those factors in mind.

But understanding the user isn't just about gathering information and being empathetic - it's also about using that information to inform the design process. This means making decisions based on user needs and preferences, and testing and iterating on designs to ensure that they meet those needs.

In the end, understanding the user is all about creating products that people love and appreciate. It's about designing with empathy and consideration for their needs, desires, and behaviors. And just like how a successful first date can lead to a great relationship, understanding the user can lead to a successful product that meets the needs and desires of its users.

Identifying user needs

Identifying user needs is like detective work - you need to gather clues, ask questions, and piece together the puzzle of what your users really want and need. Just like how a detective needs to be thorough and methodical, product designers need to approach the task of identifying user needs with care and attention to detail.

So, how do you identify user needs in product design? Here are some key steps:

1. **Conduct User Research:** Start by conducting user research. This can involve surveys, interviews, focus

groups, and other methods of gathering information about your users. Ask open-ended questions to uncover their needs, desires, and pain points.

2. **Observe User Behavior:** Another important aspect of identifying user needs is observing how users interact with your product. This can involve usability testing, where users try out a prototype of the product and provide feedback on their experience. By watching how users interact with the product, designers can identify areas where the product falls short or could be improved.

3. **Empathize with Users:** Empathy is key to identifying user needs. Put yourself in your users' shoes and try to see things from their perspective. Consider their emotions, motivations, and goals, and design with those factors in mind.

4. **Use Data to Inform Design Decisions:** Once you've gathered information and observed user behavior, it's time to analyze that data and use it to inform the design process. This means

identifying patterns and themes in user feedback and using that information to make design decisions that prioritize user needs and desires.

5. **Iterate:** Finally, it's important to iterate on your designs based on user feedback. Test your product with users and make changes based on their feedback. This will help ensure that your product truly meets their needs and desires.

In the end, identifying user needs is all about creating products that truly meet the needs and desires of users. It's about being thorough, methodical, and empathetic in the research process, and using that information to inform design decisions that prioritize the user experience. By doing so, designers can create products that users truly love and appreciate.

Conducting user research

User research is like a treasure hunt - you need to follow clues, search for answers, and uncover hidden gems of information that can inform your design decisions. Just like how a treasure hunter needs a map and a plan, product designers need to approach user research with a clear strategy and a set of tools and techniques to gather insights about their users.

Conducting user research is an essential part of the product design process. It allows designers to gather information about their users, their needs, and their pain points, which can then be used to inform the design of the product. Here are some steps to help you conduct user research effectively:

- **Define your research goals:** Before you start conducting user research, you need to define your goals. What are you trying to learn about your users? What questions do you want to answer? Having clear research goals will help you focus your research efforts and make the most of your time and resources.

- **Choose your research methods:** There are many different methods you can use to conduct user research, including surveys, interviews, focus groups, and usability testing. Choose the methods that are best suited to your research goals and budget. For example, if you want to get in-depth information about your users' experiences, interviews might be the best option.

- **Recruit participants:** Once you've chosen your research methods, you need to recruit participants. Consider the demographics of your target audience and choose participants who are representative of that group. You can recruit participants through social media, email lists, or by using a recruitment agency.

- **Conduct your research:** When it's time to conduct your research, make sure you have a clear plan in place. Use open-ended questions to encourage participants to share their thoughts and experiences. Take detailed notes during interviews and focus groups, and record usability testing sessions so you can review them later.

- **Analyze your findings:** After you've conducted your research, it's time to analyze your findings. Look for patterns and themes in the data, and use that information to inform your design decisions. For example, if many participants mentioned that they had difficulty using a particular feature, that's a sign that the feature needs to be redesigned.

- **Iterate:** Finally, it's important to iterate on your designs based on the feedback you receive from user research. Test your designs with users and make changes based on their feedback. This will help ensure that your product truly meets the needs of your users.

Overall, conducting user research is a crucial part of the product design process. By defining your research goals, choosing the right methods, recruiting participants, conducting your research, analyzing your findings, and iterating on your designs, you can create products that truly meet the needs of your users.
Conducting user research is all about gaining insights into your users and using that information to create products that truly meet their needs and desires. By following a clear research plan and being empathetic and open-minded, designers

can gather the insights they need to create products that users will love.

Creating user personas

Creating user personas is a helpful tool in product design to help designers better understand their users. User personas are fictional representations of your target users, based on research and data, that can help you make design decisions that cater to the needs and goals of your users. Here are some steps to help you create user personas effectively:

- **Conduct user research:** Before you can create user personas, you need to conduct user research. This can include surveys, interviews, and observation to gather information about your users, their needs, goals, and behaviors. This information will serve as the basis for creating your user personas.

- **Identify common patterns:** After conducting your user research, identify common patterns and themes in the data. For example, you may find that a significant portion of your users are working parents with busy schedules who are looking for time-saving solutions. Oftentimes, it includes demographics like age, gender, and occupation, as well as behavioral information such as pain points, goals, and habits.

- **Create user persona profiles:** Using the patterns and themes identified in your research, create fictional user persona profiles that represent your target users. Each persona should have a name, age, occupation, personality traits, and information about their job, family life, and hobbies. It is also imperative to have a brief background story that reflects the goals, behaviors, and motivations of your users.

- **Add details:** To make your personas more realistic, add details such as photos, quotes, and anecdotes. This will help you and your team better empathize with your users and understand their needs.

- **Use your personas to inform design decisions:** Once you have created your user personas, you can use them to inform your design decisions. For example, if one of your user personas is a working parent with a busy schedule, you may want to design features that help them save time and manage their schedule more effectively. You can ask questions like "How would this feature help or hinder Persona A in achieving their goals?" or "Would Persona B find this design intuitive?"

- **Keep your personas up to date:** It's important to keep your user personas up to date as your user base evolves and your product changes. Revisit your user personas periodically to ensure that they still accurately represent your users' needs and behaviors.

Creating user personas can help you gain a better understanding of your users and make design decisions that cater to their needs and goals. By conducting user research, identifying common patterns, creating user persona profiles, using your personas to inform design decisions, and keeping your personas up to date, you can create products that truly meet the needs of your users.

User experience design

User experience design (UX design) is a critical component of product design. At its core, UX design is all about creating products that meet the needs of users in a way that is intuitive and enjoyable to use. Let's explore some of the key concepts and principles of UX design:

User-centered design: User-centered design is a critical principle in product design, and it's at the heart of creating a successful user experience. At its core, user-centered design is all about understanding the needs of your users and designing products that meet those needs. This might seem like an obvious concept, but it's surprising how many products are designed without considering the user's perspective. The first step in user-centered design is to understand your users. This involves conducting user research to gain insights into their needs, motivations, and behaviors. Once you have a solid understanding of your users, you can start designing products that meet their needs.

It's important to remember that user-centered design isn't just about designing products that users want – it's about designing products that they need. This requires a deep understanding of your users and their goals. You need to understand their pain points, their frustrations, and their motivations in order to create a product that truly meets their needs. User-centered design also involves testing and iterating on your designs based on user feedback. This means conducting user testing to see how your product performs in the hands of real users. User testing can help you identify pain points and areas for improvement, so that you can make changes and improve the user experience. One of the key benefits of user-centered design is that it helps you create products that are more likely to succeed in the market. By designing products that meet the needs of your users, you can create products that are more useful, more usable, and more enjoyable to use. This can help you gain a competitive edge in the market, as users will be more likely to choose your product over others.

In conclusion, user-centered design is a critical principle in product design. By understanding the needs of your users and designing products that meet those needs, you can create products that are more likely to succeed in the market. So the next time you're designing a product, remember to put your users at the center of your design process.

Usability: At its core, usability is all about how easy and efficient it is for users to achieve their goals with your product. When users interact with your product, they want to be able to accomplish their tasks quickly and easily. If they struggle to use your product, they're likely to become frustrated and may even abandon it altogether.

To create a product that is highly usable, you need to consider a wide range of factors. One of the most important is the layout and navigation of your product. Your product should be designed in a way that is intuitive and easy to understand. Users should be able to navigate your product without confusion, and they should be able to find what they're looking for quickly and easily.

Another important factor to consider is the language and tone of your content. The words you use and the way you present information can have a big impact on how users perceive your product. You should strive to use clear and concise language that is easy to understand. You should also aim to create a tone that is friendly and approachable, rather than cold and formal. Usability testing is a critical part of the UX design process. This involves testing your product with real users to see how they interact with it. During usability testing, you can observe how users navigate your product, identify areas where they struggle, and make changes to improve the user experience.

By focusing on usability in your UX design, you can create products that are more enjoyable to use and more likely to succeed in the market. Users will appreciate products that are easy to use and efficient, and they're more likely to recommend them to others.

Visual design: While usability focuses on how easy and efficient it is for users to achieve their goals, visual design is all about how your product looks and feels. It includes elements such as color palettes, typography, graphics, and overall aesthetic appeal.

A well-designed product should be aesthetically pleasing and reinforce the brand identity. The colors and typography you choose should reflect your brand's personality and values. The graphics and imagery should be high-quality and visually appealing, and they should be used to support the content and enhance the user experience.

The visual design of your product should also be consistent throughout. Users should be able to recognize your product immediately based on its visual design elements. Consistency in visual design helps to create a sense of familiarity and builds trust with users.

Visual design can also play a role in guiding users through your product. By using visual cues, such as color and typography, you can draw attention to important elements and guide users through the product flow.

In addition, visual design can help to create an emotional connection with users. A well-designed product can evoke feelings of joy, excitement, or trust, which can help to build a stronger relationship between users and your product.

When it comes to visual design, it's important to strike a balance between form and function. While aesthetics are important, they should never come at the expense of usability. A beautiful product that is difficult to use will ultimately fail to meet user needs and expectations.

Visual design is a critical aspect of UX design. It includes elements such as color palettes, typography, graphics, and overall aesthetic appeal. A well-designed product should be aesthetically pleasing, consistent, and reinforce the brand identity. By striking a balance between form and function, you can create a visually appealing product that is also easy to use and meets user needs.

Accessibility: This involves ensuring that your product can be used by as many people as possible, including those with disabilities. This includes making sure that the product is usable by people with visual, auditory, and physical impairments, as well as those with cognitive and learning disabilities.

To make your product accessible, you need to consider a range of factors. For example, you may need to provide alternative text for images, so that users with visual impairments can understand what the images convey. Similarly, you may need to use clear and simple language, so that users with cognitive disabilities can understand the content.

Other factors that can impact accessibility include color contrast, font size, and navigation. For example, you may need to use high contrast colors, so that users with visual impairments can easily distinguish between different elements on the screen. You may also need to use a larger font size, so that users with visual impairments can read the content.

In addition, you may need to provide alternative ways for users to interact with your product. For example, you may need to provide keyboard shortcuts or voice commands, so that users with physical disabilities can navigate the product without using a mouse.

By making your product accessible, you can help to ensure that all users can benefit from its features and functionality. Accessibility also demonstrates a commitment to inclusivity and diversity, which can help to build a stronger relationship with your users.

In conclusion, accessibility is an important aspect of UX design. It involves making your product usable by as many people as possible, including those with disabilities. To make your product accessible, you need to consider a range of factors, such as alternative text for images, clear and simple language, color contrast, font size, and navigation. By making your product accessible, you can ensure that all users can benefit from its features and functionality, and build a stronger relationship with your users.

User feedback: It is often said that without feedback, there can be no user-centered design. Why is feedback so important? Simply put, it helps you understand how your users are interacting with your product and what their needs and pain points are. There are many ways to gather user feedback, including surveys, usability testing, focus groups, and customer support interactions. Surveys can help you gather quantitative data, such as satisfaction ratings or task completion rates. Usability testing, on the other hand, is more qualitative and involves observing users as they interact with your product and asking them to think aloud as they complete tasks. Focus groups can be useful for gathering feedback on specific features or aspects of your product, while customer support interactions can provide valuable insight into common user issues and complaints. Once you've gathered feedback, it's important to analyze and synthesize it in a way that allows you to make informed design decisions. This might involve categorizing feedback into themes, identifying trends or patterns, and prioritizing issues based on their impact on the user experience.

Ultimately, user feedback is essential for creating products that meet the needs of your target audience. By listening to your users and using their feedback to inform your design decisions, you can create products that are both usable and enjoyable to use.

An important concept in UX design is the user journey. This is the path that a user takes when interacting with your product, from initial discovery to ongoing use. By understanding the user journey, you can identify pain points and opportunities to improve the user experience.

A key principle in UX design is to keep things simple. A cluttered or confusing interface can lead to frustration and dissatisfaction among users. Instead, focus on designing products that are intuitive and easy to use.

UX design is an iterative process. This means that you'll likely need to make adjustments and improvements to your product based on user feedback and testing. Don't be afraid to try new things and take risks – just be sure to test and validate your ideas with real users.

In conclusion, UX design is an essential component of product design. By focusing on the needs and experiences of your users, you can create products that are intuitive, efficient, and enjoyable to use. So next time you're designing a product, remember to keep the user at the center of your design process.

Chapter 3: Ideation and Brainstorming

Ah, ideation and brainstorming – the exciting and creative part of product design! This is where the magic happens, where ideas are born and transformed into tangible products. But before we dive into the fun part, let's start with the basics. Ideation is the process of generating new and innovative ideas. It's where you explore various possibilities and come up with creative solutions to a problem. Brainstorming, on the other hand, is a specific technique used to generate a large number of ideas in a short period of time. Now, when it comes to ideation and brainstorming in product design, it's essential to keep in mind that creativity needs structure. It's not just about randomly spitting out ideas, but rather about having a clear understanding of the problem you're trying to solve and the needs of your users.

Anecdote time! I remember working on a product design project for a client who wanted to create a new type of fitness app. We started with a brainstorming session where we generated a bunch of ideas, from tracking workouts to social features for accountability. But it wasn't until we dug deeper into the needs and motivations of the target audience – busy professionals with little time to spare – that we came up with the winning idea: a quick and efficient 15-minute workout program.

So, where do you begin with ideation and brainstorming in product design? First, you need to define the problem you're trying to solve. What is the pain point or challenge your product aims to address? Then, gather a diverse team of individuals with different backgrounds and perspectives to bring a variety of ideas to the table.

During the brainstorming process, it's essential to suspend judgment and encourage wild and crazy ideas. You never know what will spark the next big thing! Once you have a list of ideas, you can narrow down the options based on feasibility, impact, and alignment with user needs.

Incorporating ideation and brainstorming into your product design process can lead to exciting and innovative solutions. And with a structured approach, you can ensure that the ideas generated are both creative and practical. So go ahead, let your imagination run wild – you never know where it might take you!

Generating and refining ideas

Generating and refining ideas is a crucial aspect of the product design process. It involves coming up with innovative and creative solutions to meet the needs of your users, and then refining those ideas until they are viable and practical to implement. The first step in generating ideas is to have a brainstorming session. This can be done with a team of designers or individually. The key is to have an open mind and encourage creativity. There are many different techniques that can be used to facilitate brainstorming, such as mind mapping, word association, or even drawing.

Once you have a list of ideas, the next step is to refine them. This involves evaluating each idea based on factors such as feasibility, market demand, and user needs. Some ideas may be discarded at this stage, while others may be combined or developed further.

One useful technique for refining ideas is called the "6-3-5 Method." In this technique, a group of six individuals generates three ideas each in five minutes. The ideas are then passed to the next person, who builds on them or generates new ones. This process continues until all six individuals have contributed to each idea.

Another important aspect of refining ideas is to get feedback from users. This can be done through user testing, surveys, or focus groups. By gathering feedback, you can identify which ideas resonate with your users and which ones need further refinement.

It's also important to consider the feasibility of your ideas. This includes factors such as cost, technology, and resources. Some ideas may be too expensive or difficult to implement, while others may require new technology or expertise.

Ultimately, the goal of generating and refining ideas is to come up with a set of concepts that can be prototyped and tested with users. This allows you to evaluate the effectiveness of your ideas and make any necessary adjustments before launching the product.

In summary, generating and refining ideas is a crucial aspect of the product design process. It requires creativity, open-mindedness, and the ability to evaluate ideas based on feasibility and user needs. Through techniques such as brainstorming, the 6-3-5 Method, and user testing, designers can come up with innovative and effective solutions to meet the needs of their users.

Methods for brainstorming

Brainstorming – the creative process that is both exhilarating and terrifying. It's the part of product design where you get to throw out wild and crazy ideas and hope that something sticks. But sometimes, it can feel like you're just staring at a blank page, waiting for inspiration to strike. Fear not, my friend! In this chapter, we'll explore some methods for brainstorming in product design that can help you generate a plethora of ideas.

Brainstorming is a crucial part of the ideation process, and it involves generating a large number of ideas in a short period of time. These ideas can then be refined and evaluated to identify the best ones for further development. Let's take a look at some popular methods for brainstorming:

- **Mind Mapping:** Mind mapping is a technique for visually organizing information. It involves writing down a central idea and then brainstorming related ideas around it, creating a "map" of interconnected thoughts. This method can help generate a large number of ideas and allows for easy organization and categorization.

- **SCAMPER:** SCAMPER is an acronym that stands for Substitute, Combine, Adapt, Modify, Put to another use, Eliminate, and Rearrange. This method involves applying each of these prompts to an existing product or idea to generate new ideas. For example, you might substitute a different material, combine two features, or eliminate a problematic element.

- **Brainwriting:** Brainwriting is a group brainstorming method where individuals write down their ideas on a sheet of paper for a set amount of time before passing the paper to the next person. This method allows for a larger number of ideas to be generated in a short amount of time, and it can also encourage more diverse perspectives.

- **Round Robin:** In a round-robin brainstorming session, each person in a group takes a turn contributing an idea. This method ensures that everyone has an equal opportunity to share their thoughts and can lead to more collaboration and engagement.

- **Rapid Ideation:** Rapid ideation involves generating a large number of ideas in a short amount of time, typically using a timer. This method encourages free-flowing creativity and can help prevent individuals from getting too attached to a single idea.

- **Analogies:** Using analogies involves comparing a problem or idea to something unrelated to spark creative thinking. For example, if you are trying to design a new kitchen gadget, you might compare it to a Swiss Army Knife or a Rubik's Cube to generate new ideas.

Once you've generated a bunch of ideas, it's time to start refining them. This is where you evaluate your ideas based on feasibility, desirability, and viability. Feasibility refers to whether or not your idea is technically possible. Desirability refers to whether or not it meets the needs of your users. And viability refers to whether or not it makes sense from a business standpoint.

One tool you can use to evaluate your ideas is a "decision matrix." This involves creating a table with criteria for evaluation, such as feasibility, desirability, and viability, and assigning each criterion a weight based on its importance. Then, you can score each idea on each criterion and calculate a total score to determine which ideas are worth pursuing.

Remember, the ideation and brainstorming phase is all about being open to new and crazy ideas. Don't be afraid to think outside the box and challenge yourself to come up with something truly innovative. And who knows – maybe that wild and crazy idea will turn out to be the next big thing.

Idea selection and prioritization

This is the often-dreaded but always-necessary step in product design. This is where you take all those great ideas generated during brainstorming and whittle them down to a manageable few. But how do you do that? Let's dive in and explore some methods for idea selection and prioritization.

First and foremost, you need to define your selection criteria. What are the most important factors to consider when selecting ideas? Some common criteria include feasibility, impact, alignment with business goals, and customer value. Once you have your criteria defined, you can begin to evaluate each idea.

One method for evaluating ideas is the "weighted scoring" approach. This involves assigning a score to each idea based on how well it meets your defined criteria. For example, you might assign a higher score to an idea that is both feasible and aligned with your business goals, while assigning a lower score to an idea that is only feasible but doesn't align with your goals. Once you have scored each idea, you can add up the scores and compare them to determine which ideas are most promising.

So you've generated a ton of great ideas through brainstorming, but now what? How do you choose which ideas to move forward with and prioritize? Let's cover some methods for idea selection and prioritization to help you choose the best ideas for your product.

- **Method 1: Feasibility**
  One important factor to consider when selecting and prioritizing ideas is feasibility. Can the idea be realistically executed given your resources, time frame, and other constraints? It's important to evaluate the feasibility of each idea before moving forward with it. This can save you time and resources in the long run.

- **Method 2: Impact**
  Another important factor to consider is the impact that each idea will have on your users and your business. Will it solve a key pain point for your users? Will it help your business achieve its goals? Prioritizing ideas based on impact can help ensure that you're focusing on the most important ideas.

- **Method 3: User Feedback**

User feedback is also a valuable tool for idea selection and prioritization. Gather feedback from potential users on each idea to gauge their interest and whether it would solve a problem for them. This can help you identify the most promising ideas.

- **Method 4: Cost-Benefit Analysis**
A cost-benefit analysis is a tool used to evaluate the potential costs and benefits of each idea. This can help you make informed decisions about which ideas to prioritize. Consider the potential costs of implementing each idea, as well as the potential benefits to your users and your business.

- **Method 5: Prioritization Matrix**
A prioritization matrix is a tool that can help you prioritize ideas based on multiple factors. Create a matrix with each idea listed, and assign a score to each idea based on factors such as feasibility, impact, and cost. Then, rank the ideas based on their total score to prioritize them.

Selecting and prioritizing ideas is a crucial step in the product design process. By considering factors such as feasibility, impact, user feedback, cost-benefit analysis, and using a prioritization matrix, you can choose the best ideas for your product. Remember to be open to feedback and willing to make changes as needed to ensure that your product is meeting the needs of your users and your business.

Creating concept sketches and storyboards

This is the bread and butter of product design! If you're looking to bring your ideas to life, then these two techniques are the perfect place to start.

Concept sketches are simple, quick drawings that allow you to explore different design ideas and concepts. These sketches are usually rough, with minimal details and annotations, but they can be incredibly helpful when it comes to visualizing your ideas and communicating them to others. Think of concept sketches like a brainstorming session on paper. The goal is to get as many ideas out as possible, without worrying too much about the details. It's a great way to explore different design directions and see what works and what doesn't.

Once you have some solid ideas down on paper, it's time to move onto storyboarding. Storyboarding is essentially the process of creating a visual narrative that tells the story of how a user would interact with your product. It's like creating a comic strip for your product!

Storyboarding is a critical step in the product design process because it allows you to see how users will engage with your product in a real-world setting. It also allows you to identify any potential issues or areas for improvement before you move onto the prototyping stage.

To create a storyboard, you'll want to start by outlining the main user flows and scenarios that you want to illustrate. Then, sketch out each scene, including the user, the environment, and any important details. Finally, annotate each scene with notes about what's happening and what the user is doing.

Both concept sketches and storyboards can be incredibly powerful tools for product designers. They allow you to explore different design ideas, communicate your vision to others, and identify any potential issues before you start building. So grab a pencil and paper, and start sketching!

Chapter 4: Prototyping and Testing

This is the exciting stage of product design where you get to see your ideas come to life! This chapter is all about bringing your concepts to reality through prototyping and putting them to the test with user feedback. Prototyping and testing are critical components of the product design process, allowing designers to evaluate the usability and effectiveness of their ideas before they are launched to the market. Prototyping involves creating a physical or digital model of the product, while testing involves observing users as they interact with the prototype and collecting feedback to inform further design decisions. In this chapter we'll dive into the importance of prototyping and testing in product design, as well as some common techniques and best practices for creating prototypes and conducting tests. So, grab a pen and paper, and let's get prototyping!

The importance of prototyping

Prototyping is a critical component of the product design process. It involves creating a preliminary model or sample of a product to test and evaluate its features, functionalities, and user experience. Prototyping allows designers to get a better understanding of how their ideas work in practice, identify areas for improvement, and make necessary changes before launching the final product.

One of the key benefits of prototyping is that it provides an opportunity to get feedback from users and stakeholders early on in the design process. This feedback can help designers make informed decisions about the product's features, usability, and overall user experience.

Another advantage of prototyping is that it helps designers identify and address technical issues before the final product is launched. By testing various iterations of the product, designers can ensure that it functions as intended, is easy to use, and meets the needs of its target audience.

Prototyping also allows for experimentation and innovation. Designers can try out new ideas and explore different design solutions without committing to a final product design. This flexibility can lead to creative breakthroughs and unexpected insights that improve the final product.

Finally, prototyping helps to mitigate risk. By testing and refining a product through prototyping, designers can minimize the risk of failure or costly mistakes. This is particularly important in industries where the cost of failure is high, such as healthcare or aviation.

Prototyping is a crucial part of the product design process, and there are many benefits to creating prototypes before finalizing a product design. Here are a few of the most significant benefits:

- **Identifying flaws and issues:** Prototyping allows designers to identify any flaws or issues with a design before it goes into production. By testing a prototype, designers can see what works and what doesn't, and make adjustments to improve the design.

- **Gathering user feedback:** Prototypes can be used to gather feedback from users, which can help designers understand how people will interact with the product and what changes need to be made. This feedback can be used to refine the design and create a better user experience.

- **Saving time and money:** Creating a prototype can actually save time and money in the long run. By identifying flaws early on, designers can make changes before production begins, which can save time and money down the line.

- **Encouraging collaboration:** Prototyping can encourage collaboration between designers, engineers, and other stakeholders. By working together to create a prototype, team members can share ideas and insights, which can lead to a better overall design.

- **Building excitement:** Prototypes can be used to generate excitement and build anticipation for a new product. Showing a prototype to potential customers or investors can help them visualize the final product and generate interest in it.

By creating prototypes, designers can identify flaws, gather user feedback, save time and money, encourage collaboration, and build excitement for a new product. Overall, prototyping is a vital component of the product design process that allows designers to test and refine their ideas, get feedback from users, and mitigate risks. By investing time and resources into prototyping, designers can create products that are more effective, efficient, and user-friendly.

Types of prototypes

Prototyping allows designers to create tangible representations of their ideas, test them, and iterate upon them. In this chapter, we'll discuss the various types of prototypes that are commonly used in product design.

- **Paper Prototypes:** Paper prototypes are the simplest form of prototyping, and they involve sketching out the design of a product on paper. Paper prototypes can be created quickly and inexpensively and are great for early-stage ideation and testing.

- **Low-Fidelity Prototypes:** Low-fidelity prototypes are rough mockups of a product that are created using basic materials such as cardboard, foam, or clay. These prototypes are useful for testing the basic functionality and usability of a product.

- **Interactive Prototypes:** Interactive prototypes are digital simulations of a product that allow users to interact with the design. These prototypes can be created using software tools like Adobe XD, Sketch, or Figma. Interactive prototypes are useful for testing the user experience and functionality of a product.

- **High-Fidelity Prototypes:** High-fidelity prototypes are fully functional, pixel-perfect replicas of a product. They are often created using code and programming languages and can be used to test the performance and functionality of a product in a real-world environment.

- **Functional Prototypes:** Functional prototypes are physical prototypes that are created using materials such as plastic, metal, or wood. These prototypes are fully functional and can be used to test the mechanical and electrical components of a product.

Each type of prototype has its benefits and drawbacks, and the choice of which type to use will depend on the specific needs of the design project. By using the appropriate type of prototype, designers can test and refine their ideas, leading to better products that meet the needs of their users.

Testing prototypes with users

When it comes to product design, it's crucial to test prototypes with users to ensure that the final product meets their needs and expectations. In this chapter, we'll dive into the importance of testing prototypes with users, how to conduct user testing, and some best practices for getting the most out of your testing sessions.
First things first, why is testing prototypes with users so important? Well, it's because user testing can help you identify potential issues and opportunities for improvement

before your product is released to the market. By observing how users interact with your prototype, you can gain valuable insights into their behavior, preferences, and pain points. This information can then be used to refine and improve your product before it's too late.

Now, let's talk about how to conduct user testing. There are several different methods you can use, including usability testing, A/B testing, and surveys. Usability testing involves observing users as they perform tasks with your prototype, while A/B testing compares the performance of different versions of your prototype. Surveys can also be useful for gathering feedback from a large number of users.

When conducting user testing, it's important to have a clear plan in place. You'll need to define your goals and objectives, as well as the tasks that users will be asked to perform. You should also consider the demographic of your user testing group and ensure that it represents your target audience.

During the testing process, it's important to remain objective and avoid leading users towards certain behaviors or conclusions. Encourage participants to think aloud and ask open-ended questions to gather their feedback. You should also take detailed notes and record the testing session for later analysis.

Once you've completed the user testing, it's time to analyze the results and use them to improve your prototype. Look for patterns in user behavior and feedback and use this information to make informed design decisions. It's also important to prioritize the changes that will have the greatest impact on user experience.

In summary, testing prototypes with users is a crucial step in the product design process. It allows you to gather valuable feedback and insights, identify potential issues and opportunities for improvement, and refine your prototype to better meet the needs and expectations of your target audience. So, be sure to incorporate user testing into your design process and use the results to create a product that truly delights your users!

Testing prototypes with users is an important step in the product design process. It helps to identify usability issues and ensure that the product meets the needs of its target audience. Here are some tips on how to effectively test prototypes with users:

- **Identify your target audience:** Before you start testing, it's important to identify who your target audience is. Who are the people who will be using your product? What are their needs and expectations?

- **Develop a test plan:** Once you know your target audience, develop a plan for testing. What tasks do you want users to perform with the prototype? What questions do you want to ask them? How will you record their responses?

- **Recruit participants:** Recruit participants who match your target audience. This can be done through social media, online communities, or by reaching out to friends and family.

- **Set up a testing environment:** Set up a testing environment that is comfortable and free of distractions. Provide any necessary equipment, such as a computer or tablet, and make sure the prototype is easy to access.

- **Provide instructions:** Provide clear instructions on how to use the prototype and what tasks to perform. Encourage participants to think aloud and share their thoughts as they interact with the prototype.

- **Observe and record:** Observe participants as they use the prototype and record their actions and feedback. Take note of any usability issues or areas for improvement.

- **Analyze results:** Once testing is complete, analyze the results to identify common themes and issues. Use this information to refine the prototype and make improvements.

Testing prototypes with users can be a valuable part of the product design process. It helps to ensure that the product meets the needs of its target audience and is easy to use. By following these tips, you can effectively test your prototypes and make informed design decisions.

Iterating on designs based on feedback

In product design, iteration is the process of refining and improving your design based on feedback from users. It's all about taking what you've learned from testing your prototypes and using that knowledge to make your product even better.

The goal of iteration is to create a design that meets the needs of your users and provides the best possible experience. It's a crucial part of the design process, as it allows you to fine-tune your design until it's just right.

There are a few key steps to the iteration process:

- **Analyze feedback:** The first step in iteration is to carefully analyze the feedback you've received from users. Look for patterns and common themes in the feedback, and identify areas where users are struggling or expressing frustration.

- **Generate ideas:** Based on the feedback you've received, brainstorm ideas for how you can improve your design.

Consider both big changes and small tweaks that can make a big impact.

- **Prototype:** Once you have some ideas for how to improve your design, create new prototypes that reflect those changes. Test those prototypes with users to see if they are effective in addressing the issues identified in the feedback.

- **Test:** Test your new prototypes with users to see how they respond. Take notes and pay close attention to their reactions, as this will give you valuable insight into how well your changes are working.

- **Repeat:** Continue this process of analyzing feedback, generating ideas, prototyping, and testing until you have a design that meets the needs of your users and provides the best possible experience.

It's important to note that iteration is not a linear process. You may need to revisit earlier steps as you receive new feedback and generate new ideas. That's perfectly normal, and in fact, it's a sign that you're truly committed to creating the best possible design.

So don't be afraid to iterate! Embrace the process, and use feedback from users to guide your design decisions. With each iteration, you'll be one step closer to creating a product that truly meets the needs of your users.

Chapter 5: Designing for Manufacturing

Welcome to the exciting world of designing for manufacturing! When it comes to product design, it's not enough to simply create a beautiful and functional prototype. To make your product a reality, you need to consider how it will be manufactured on a large scale. This means taking into account materials, production processes, and assembly methods from the very beginning of the design process.

Designing for manufacturing requires a careful balance between creativity and practicality. You want your product to stand out from the competition and capture the hearts of your customers, but you also need to ensure that it can be manufactured efficiently and cost-effectively.

In this chapter, we'll explore the various considerations that go into designing for manufacturing, from choosing materials to optimizing production processes. We'll discuss the importance of collaboration between designers and manufacturers, and share tips and best practices for creating designs that can be easily brought to life on the assembly line. So, let's dive in and explore the exciting world of manufacturing-focused product design!

Design considerations for manufacturing

When it comes to product design, creating a product that is aesthetically pleasing and functional is only half the battle. The next step is to make sure that your product can actually be manufactured efficiently and effectively. This is where design considerations for manufacturing come into play.

Designing for manufacturing involves taking into account various factors such as the materials used, the production process, and the cost of production. Here are some design considerations to keep in mind:

- **Material Selection:** The choice of material can greatly impact the ease of manufacturing and the cost. When selecting materials, consider factors such as availability, cost, durability, and recyclability. It's also important to consider the properties of the material, such as strength and flexibility, and how it will hold up over time.

- **Design for Assembly:** The way that components fit together can greatly impact the ease of assembly and the time required for production. When designing a product, consider how the components will be assembled and how they will be secured together. Designs that are easy to assemble will reduce production time and cost.

- **Design for Manufacturability:** It's important to design products that can be easily and efficiently manufactured. Consider the production process and identify potential challenges that may arise. For example, if a product requires multiple parts to be assembled, it may be more efficient to design those parts as one piece to reduce assembly time and cost.

- **Cost Reduction:** One of the biggest considerations in manufacturing is cost. Designing products with cost in mind can help reduce the overall cost of production. Consider ways to reduce material usage, simplify the manufacturing process, and reduce assembly time.

- **Quality Control:** It's important to design products with quality control in mind. This means designing products that are reliable and consistent in their performance. This can be achieved through design features such as standardized components, clear assembly instructions, and consistent manufacturing processes.

Designing for manufacturing can be a complex process, but by considering these factors, you can create products that are not only aesthetically pleasing and functional, but also efficient and cost-effective to produce.

Working with suppliers and manufacturers

When it comes to bringing your product design to life, working with suppliers and manufacturers is a crucial part of the process. While you may have a great design in mind, the practicalities of manufacturing can present their own unique challenges. Here are some tips on how to work effectively with suppliers and manufacturers to ensure that your product is successfully produced.

Firstly, it's important to research and identify potential suppliers and manufacturers that are capable of producing your product. Look for companies that have experience in producing similar products and that have a good reputation for quality and reliability.

Once you have identified potential suppliers and manufacturers, it's important to communicate your design and specifications clearly and effectively. Provide detailed drawings and technical specifications, and be open to feedback and suggestions from the manufacturer. This can help ensure that the manufacturing process is as smooth and efficient as possible.

Another key consideration when working with suppliers and manufacturers is cost. Be transparent about your budget and negotiate pricing that is fair for both parties. Keep in mind that there may be additional costs for tooling, setup, and other manufacturing processes, so be sure to factor these into your budget.

It's also important to establish clear communication channels with your suppliers and manufacturers. This can include regular progress updates, production timelines, and quality control measures. By maintaining open and frequent communication, you can help ensure that the manufacturing process stays on track and any issues are identified and addressed in a timely manner.

Finally, it's important to build strong relationships with your suppliers and manufacturers. This can include regular visits to their facilities, attending industry events, and providing feedback on their performance. By building trust and rapport, you can create a long-term partnership that benefits both parties.

In summary, working with suppliers and manufacturers is a crucial part of the product design process. By researching and identifying potential partners, communicating clearly and effectively, negotiating pricing, establishing clear communication channels, and building strong relationships, you can help ensure that your product is successfully produced and meets your design specifications.

Materials selection and manufacturing processes

When it comes to designing a product, choosing the right materials and manufacturing processes can make all the difference. Not only can it impact the final appearance and functionality of the product, but it can also affect its cost and environmental impact. In this chapter, we will explore the importance of materials selection and manufacturing processes in product design, and how they can be optimized to create the best possible outcome.

Materials Selection: Choosing the right materials for a product is crucial. The materials used can affect the durability, functionality, and aesthetic appeal of the final product. For instance, if you're designing a phone case, you might consider using a durable material such as polycarbonate, which can withstand scratches and drops, and provides a good grip for the user. Alternatively, if you're designing a high-end watch, you might choose to use a more luxurious material like stainless steel or even gold.

When selecting materials, designers must also consider factors such as sustainability and environmental impact. In recent years, consumers have become increasingly aware of the impact that their purchases have on the environment, and are demanding more sustainable and eco-friendly options. Thus, designers must keep this in mind when selecting materials for their products. Some examples of sustainable materials include bamboo, recycled plastics, and organic cotton.

Manufacturing Processes: The manufacturing process used to create a product can also have a significant impact on its final outcome. For instance, a product that is mass-produced using injection molding will have a different look and feel than one that is made using CNC machining. Additionally, the manufacturing process can also affect the cost of the final product. When choosing a manufacturing process, designers must consider factors such as cost, efficiency, and scalability. For instance, if you're creating a limited-edition product, you might choose to use a more artisanal manufacturing process, such as hand-crafting. However, if you're creating a product that will be sold in large quantities, you might need to use a more automated process to keep costs down and ensure efficiency.

Working with Suppliers and Manufacturers: Designers must also work closely with suppliers and manufacturers to ensure that their product is produced to the desired quality and specifications. This involves working with vendors to select the right materials, negotiating pricing, and overseeing the production process to ensure that everything is running smoothly. It's important to maintain open communication with suppliers and manufacturers throughout the process, to ensure that any issues are addressed quickly and efficiently. This can help to avoid costly mistakes and delays, and ensure that the final product meets the desired specifications.

Materials selection and manufacturing processes are critical components of product design. By carefully selecting the right materials and manufacturing processes, and working closely with suppliers and manufacturers, designers can create products that are functional, aesthetically pleasing, and environmentally sustainable.

Design for assembly and disassembly

Design for assembly and disassembly is an important consideration in product design. It refers to the process of designing a product in a way that makes it easy to assemble during manufacturing and disassemble for repair, maintenance, or recycling at the end of its life cycle. In this chapter, we will explore the importance of designing for assembly and disassembly and the various factors that should be taken into consideration.

One of the primary benefits of designing for assembly is that it can significantly reduce manufacturing costs. By making a product easier to assemble, manufacturers can save time and resources, resulting in lower production costs. This, in turn, can translate into lower prices for consumers and increased competitiveness for the company.

On the other hand, designing for disassembly can help reduce the environmental impact of a product. When a product is designed with disassembly in mind, it becomes easier to recycle or dispose of at the end of its life cycle. This reduces the amount of waste generated by the product and helps to promote sustainable practices.

When designing for assembly and disassembly, there are several factors that need to be considered. These include the choice of materials, the manufacturing processes, the product design, and the tools required for assembly and disassembly.

The choice of materials is an essential consideration when designing for assembly and disassembly. Materials that are easy to work with and can be easily disassembled are preferred. For example, plastic snap-together parts are much easier to assemble and disassemble than those that require glue or adhesives.

Manufacturing processes also play a crucial role in designing for assembly and disassembly. Manufacturers must consider the number of steps involved in assembling the product and how they can be streamlined to reduce production time and costs.

The product design itself is another important consideration when designing for assembly and disassembly. Products that are modular and have fewer parts are generally easier to assemble and disassemble. Additionally, products that have clear instructions and labeling for assembly and disassembly can be helpful for both manufacturers and end-users. Finally, the tools required for assembly and disassembly should also be taken into consideration. Designers should ensure that the tools needed for assembly and disassembly are widely available and easy to use. This can help reduce the likelihood of errors during the assembly process and improve the overall user experience.

In conclusion, designing for assembly and disassembly is an essential consideration in product design. By making products easier to assemble and disassemble, manufacturers can reduce production costs, while also promoting sustainable practices. To design for assembly and disassembly, designers must consider the choice of materials, manufacturing processes, product design, and tools required for assembly and disassembly.

Chapter 6: Design for Sustainability

Design for sustainability is a growing field in product design, which emphasizes creating products that have minimal negative impact on the environment and promote sustainability. As consumers become more aware of the impact their purchasing decisions have on the planet, companies are recognizing the importance of creating sustainable products. Designers are playing a crucial role in this shift, as they have the power to create products that are not only functional and aesthetically pleasing, but also environmentally friendly. In this chapter, we will explore the principles of design for sustainability and how they can be applied to product design. We will also discuss the benefits of designing for sustainability, both for the environment and for businesses. So, let's dive in and see how we can make a positive impact through sustainable design!

The importance of sustainability in product design

It's becoming more and more important for companies to prioritize sustainability in their designs. Not only is it better for the environment, but it can also save money in the long run and improve a company's reputation. Here are some reasons why sustainability in product design is so important:

- **Environmental impact:** The products we create can have a significant impact on the environment. By designing products that are sustainable, we can minimize their negative impact and even make a positive impact.

- **Cost savings:** Sustainable designs can also save money in the long run. For example, using renewable energy sources or designing products that are more durable can reduce energy and material costs over time.

- **Reputation:** Companies that prioritize sustainability can improve their reputation among consumers, investors, and the public. People are becoming more aware of the impact their purchases have on the environment and are more likely to support companies that are doing their part to minimize that impact.

- **Regulatory compliance:** Many governments are implementing regulations and policies to promote sustainability. By designing products with these regulations in mind, companies can avoid fines and penalties and ensure they are operating ethically and responsibly.

- **Innovation:** Sustainability can also drive innovation in product design. By finding new, more sustainable materials or manufacturing processes, companies can create products that are not only better for the environment, but also better in terms of performance and functionality.

Overall, sustainability in product design is becoming increasingly important, and for good reason. By prioritizing sustainability, companies can make a positive impact on the environment, save money, improve their reputation, comply with regulations, and drive innovation. So let's start designing for a better future!

Designing for reduced environmental impact

As we become more aware of our impact on the planet, designing products with reduced environmental impact has become increasingly important. As a product designer, it's your responsibility to consider the full life-cycle of your product, from raw materials and manufacturing to use and disposal. Here are some tips for designing with reduced environmental impact:

- **Use sustainable materials:** Consider using materials that are renewable, biodegradable, or recycled. Avoid materials that are toxic, non-recyclable, or difficult to dispose of.

- **Reduce waste:** Design your product with the goal of reducing waste. This could mean using less material, designing for disassembly or reuse, or even creating a closed-loop system where waste is recycled back into the production process.

- **Minimize energy use:** Look for ways to minimize energy use throughout the lifecycle of your product. This could mean designing for energy efficiency during use, or choosing manufacturing processes that require less energy.

- **Consider the product's end of life:** Think about what will happen to your product when it's no longer useful. Can it be easily disassembled for recycling? Can the materials be composted or biodegraded? Designing for end-of-life is an important aspect of creating a sustainable product.

- **Design for durability:** A durable product will last longer, reducing the need for frequent replacements and reducing waste. Consider using high-quality materials and designing for repairability to extend the lifespan of your product.

- **Consider the transportation impact:** Transportation can be a significant source of emissions in the product lifecycle. Design for efficient transportation, using packaging that minimizes size and weight, or considering local sourcing to reduce transportation distances.

- **Involve your users:** Encourage your users to engage in sustainable practices, such as recycling or using energy-efficient settings. Provide educational resources to help them understand the environmental impact of their product use.

Designing for reduced environmental impact is not only responsible, but it can also be innovative and cost-effective. By implementing sustainable design principles, you can create products that are not only good for the planet but also appealing to consumers who are increasingly concerned about sustainability.

Life cycle assessment and design

When designing a product, it is important to consider its entire life cycle, from the extraction of raw materials to the disposal or reuse of the product at the end of its life. This is where life cycle assessment (LCA) comes in. LCA is a tool that assesses the environmental impact of a product throughout its entire life cycle, taking into account factors such as energy and resource use, emissions, and waste. Designers can use LCA to identify areas where they can reduce the environmental impact of their product. This can involve making changes to the materials used, the manufacturing process, and the end-of-life options for the product.

One example of this is the design of the Nike Considered shoe. Nike used LCA to analyze the environmental impact of its shoes and identified areas where it could reduce that impact. The result was the Considered shoe, which was designed with environmentally preferred materials and manufacturing processes.

Design for the environment (DfE) is another important concept in product design. DfE involves designing products that are environmentally friendly throughout their entire life cycle. This can involve using recycled or biodegradable materials, designing products that are easy to repair or disassemble, and designing products that are energy-efficient.

An example of DfE in action is the iPhone. Apple has made significant strides in designing its products for reduced environmental impact. For example, the iPhone 12 uses recycled rare earth materials in its magnets and contains 99% recycled tungsten in its vibration motor. Additionally, Apple has designed its products to be easily disassembled for repair and recycling.

Incorporating LCA and DfE into product design is not only good for the environment but can also be good for business. Consumers are increasingly demanding environmentally friendly products, and companies that prioritize sustainability in their product design are more likely to attract and retain customers.

So, as a product designer, it is important to consider the entire life cycle of a product and design with sustainability in mind. By incorporating LCA and DfE into your design process, you can create products that not only meet the needs of your customers but also contribute to a healthier planet.

Social and ethical considerations

As designers, it's essential to consider not only the environmental impact of our products but also their social and ethical impact. In today's world, consumers are more conscious than ever before, and they want to know that the products they purchase are ethically made and don't harm people or communities.

There are several social and ethical considerations that designers need to keep in mind when creating products. Here are a few:

- **Labor Conditions:** It's crucial to ensure that the workers who make the products are treated fairly, paid a living wage, and have safe working conditions. Sweatshops and child labor are major concerns that designers must address.

- **Supply Chain:** The entire supply chain should be considered when designing a product. Are the materials sustainably sourced, and are they transported in an environmentally friendly way? Are the suppliers using ethical practices?

- **Cultural Sensitivity:** When designing products for global markets, it's important to be sensitive to cultural differences. Something that may be acceptable in one culture may not be in another, and designers need to be aware of these differences to avoid offending anyone.

- **Accessibility:** Products should be designed to be accessible to everyone, including those with disabilities. This includes things like designing products with larger buttons, easy-to-read instructions, and ergonomic designs.

- **End-of-Life Disposal:** Designers should also consider the end-of-life disposal of their products. Can the product be recycled or reused? Is it biodegradable? These are all essential questions that must be asked to reduce waste and minimize the impact on the environment.

By considering these social and ethical factors, designers can create products that not only meet the needs of their customers but also contribute to a better world. It's not just about making a profit; it's about creating something that adds value to society while minimizing harm.

Chapter 7: Design Tools and Software

Can you imagine designing a product without the right tools? Well, it's possible, but it would be like driving a car without power steering - possible, but a lot more work. Design tools and software can help streamline the design process, save time, and enable designers to create more complex designs. From CAD software to virtual reality tools, the possibilities are endless. In this chapter, we'll explore the different types of design tools and software available to product designers, and how they can be used to create amazing products. So, let's get started!

Overview of design tools and software

Designing a product is no easy feat, and it requires a lot of creative thinking, brainstorming, and, of course, the right tools. Fortunately, the world of product design is teeming with all sorts of design tools and software that can help you take your ideas from concept to reality.
Let's start with the classic design software that most designers are familiar with: Adobe Creative Suite. From Photoshop to

Illustrator, these software programs have been a staple in the design world for years, and for good reason. They're user-friendly, versatile, and they can help you create everything from logos to packaging designs. But as technology advances, new design tools are emerging that are changing the game. One of those tools is Sketch, a design software that's gained popularity in recent years. Sketch is perfect for creating wireframes, user interfaces, and other digital designs. Its simplicity and efficiency make it a favorite among designers.

Another popular design tool is Figma, a cloud-based design platform that allows multiple designers to work on the same project in real-time. This is particularly useful for collaborative projects, as it eliminates the need for multiple versions of the same design file.

And let's not forget about the more specialized design software out there. For example, Rhino is a 3D modeling software that's particularly popular among industrial designers. It allows you to create complex 3D models that can be used for everything from prototyping to manufacturing.

But here's the thing: the right design tool for you will depend on your specific needs and preferences. Some designers swear by Sketch, while others prefer Figma or Adobe Creative Suite. It's all about finding the tool that works best for you and your workflow. At the end of the day, the world of product design is constantly evolving, and new design tools and software are always emerging. So whether you're a seasoned designer or just starting out, keep your eye out for new tools that can help you bring your ideas to life. Who knows, maybe the next big thing in product design software is just around the corner!

Sketching and drawing tools

Sketching and drawing are essential skills for any product designer. They allow you to quickly explore and iterate on ideas, communicate with team members, and even sell your designs to clients. And while there's no shortage of high-tech digital drawing tools out there, sometimes nothing beats the simplicity of a good old-fashioned pencil and paper.
But let's not discount the power of technology! There are also a variety of digital drawing tools that can help you take your sketches to the next level. Let's take a

closer look at some of the most popular sketching and drawing tools in product design:

- **Pencils:** Pencils are the classic tool for sketching and drawing, and for good reason. They're affordable, versatile, and allow you to easily adjust your lines and shading. Plus, there's something satisfying about the feel of a pencil on paper. Many product designers prefer to sketch with a 0.5 or 0.7 mm mechanical pencil for precision.

- **Markers:** Markers are another popular tool for sketching and drawing in product design. They come in a variety of colors and tip sizes, allowing you to add depth and dimension to your sketches. Many designers use markers in combination with pencils to create dynamic sketches that are both precise and expressive.

- **Tablet and Stylus:** Digital drawing tablets like the Wacom Intuos and the iPad Pro with an Apple Pencil have become increasingly popular among product designers. They allow you to create digital sketches and designs with the same precision and control as traditional drawing tools, while also offering the ability to easily undo mistakes and experiment with different colors and textures.

- **Sketchbooks:** A good sketchbook is essential for any product designer. It's the place where you can let your ideas flow freely and without judgment. Whether you prefer a small pocket-sized notebook or a larger sketchbook, make sure to choose one with high-quality paper that can handle a variety of mediums.

- **Design Software:** Finally, there's a variety of design software that can help you take your sketches to the next level. Programs like Adobe Photoshop, Illustrator, and Procreate offer a wide range of digital drawing tools and techniques that allow you to create detailed and complex designs.

At the end of the day, the tools you choose for sketching and drawing will depend on your personal preferences and workflow.

Some designers prefer to keep it simple with pencils and paper, while others prefer the versatility of digital drawing tools. The key is to experiment with different tools and techniques to find the ones that work best for you.

CAD software

CAD software – the backbone of modern product design. If you're not familiar with CAD, it stands for Computer-Aided Design, and it's a type of software that allows designers to create detailed, precise 2D and 3D models of products. But with so many CAD software options out there, how do you know which one to choose? Let's take a closer look at some of the most popular CAD software in product design:

- **SolidWorks:** SolidWorks is one of the most popular CAD software in product design, and for good reason. It's user-friendly, versatile, and allows you to create complex 3D models with ease. It also integrates seamlessly with other design software like Adobe Creative Suite, making it a favorite among designers.

- **AutoCAD:** AutoCAD is another classic CAD software that's been around for decades. It's particularly popular among architects and engineers, but it's also widely used in product design. AutoCAD allows you to create precise 2D and 3D models and has a variety of tools and features that make it easy to collaborate with team members.

- **Fusion 360:** Fusion 360 is a newer CAD software that's gaining popularity among product designers. It's cloud-based, which means you can access your designs from anywhere with an internet connection, and it's particularly good for collaboration. Fusion 360 also has a variety of features like simulation and rendering that allow you to test and visualize your designs.

- **Rhino:** Rhino is a 3D modeling software that's particularly popular among industrial designers. It allows you to create complex 3D models that can be used for everything from prototyping to manufacturing. Rhino also has a variety of plugins that allow you to customize your workflow and add new features and tools.

- **SketchUp:** SketchUp is a 3D modeling software that's known for its simplicity and ease of use. It's particularly popular among architects and interior designers, but it's also widely used in product design. SketchUp allows you to create 3D models quickly and easily, making it a favorite among designers who value speed and efficiency.

At the end of the day, the CAD software you choose will depend on your specific needs and preferences. Some designers prefer the versatility of SolidWorks, while others prefer the simplicity of SketchUp. It's all about finding the software that works best for you and your workflow. But one thing's for sure – CAD software has revolutionized the way we design products, and it's an essential tool for any modern product designer.

3D printing and other prototyping tools

When it comes to product design, prototyping is essential for testing and refining ideas before moving into production. And while there are a variety of prototyping tools out there, 3D printing has revolutionized the way designers bring their ideas to life. Let's take a closer look at 3D printing and other prototyping tools in product design:

- **3D Printing:** 3D printing allows designers to create physical models of their designs quickly and easily. It works by using a printer to build up layers of material (like plastic, metal, or even food) based on a digital 3D model. 3D printing is particularly useful for creating complex geometries that would be difficult to produce with traditional manufacturing methods. Plus, it allows designers to test and iterate on their designs in a more cost-effective way than traditional prototyping methods.

- **Laser Cutting:** Laser cutting is another popular prototyping tool in product design. It works by using a laser to cut and etch materials like wood, acrylic, and metal based on a digital design file. Laser cutting is particularly useful for creating flat, 2D designs like product enclosures, signs, and even jewelry.

- **CNC Machining:** CNC machining is a more traditional prototyping method that uses a computer-controlled cutting tool to shape materials like metal, plastic, and wood. It's particularly useful for creating larger, more complex parts that require high precision and accuracy.

- **Mold Making:** Mold making is a prototyping method that's commonly used in manufacturing. It involves creating a mold of the desired part and then using it to produce multiple copies. Mold making is particularly useful for creating parts with intricate shapes or designs that would be difficult to produce with other prototyping methods.

- **Foam Modeling:** Foam modeling is a low-tech prototyping method that involves carving a block of foam into the desired shape using hand tools like knives and sandpaper. It's particularly useful for creating rough prototypes or mockups that can be used for testing and feedback.

At the end of the day, the prototyping tools you choose will depend on your specific needs and the complexity of your designs. 3D printing is a powerful tool for creating complex, 3D models quickly and easily, while laser cutting and foam modeling are great for creating simple, 2D designs. CNC machining and mold making are more traditional prototyping methods that are useful for creating larger, more complex parts. The key is to experiment with different prototyping methods to find the ones that work best for you and your workflow.

Chapter 8: Bringing Products to Market

Bringing a product to market – the final frontier in product design! It's the stage where you get to share your creation with the world, and hopefully make a few bucks in the process. But bringing a product to market is no small feat. It requires careful planning, execution, and a bit of luck. So, let's take a closer look at some of the most important steps in bringing a product to market:

- **Market Research:** Before you even think about bringing a product to market, it's important to conduct market research. This involves researching your target audience, understanding their needs, and analyzing the competition. You'll want to gather as much data as possible to inform your product development process.

- **Design and Prototyping:** Once you have a good understanding of your market, it's time to start designing and prototyping your product. This stage involves creating physical and digital prototypes, testing them with potential customers, and refining your design based on feedback.

- **Manufacturing:** Once you have a final design, it's time to start thinking about manufacturing. This involves finding a manufacturer, negotiating pricing and production timelines, and creating a production plan. You'll also need to ensure that your product meets any regulatory requirements and industry standards.

- **Marketing and Branding:** With your product in production, it's time to start thinking about marketing and branding. This involves developing a brand identity, creating marketing materials, and building a marketing campaign to promote your product. You'll also need to think about packaging design and how to effectively showcase your product on store shelves or online marketplaces.

- **Distribution and Sales:** Finally, it's time to get your product into the hands of customers. This involves setting up a distribution network, negotiating with retailers and distributors, and building relationships with online marketplaces like Amazon or Etsy. You'll also need to have a plan for tracking sales and inventory, as well as managing customer support and returns.

Bringing a product to market is a complex and challenging process, but it's also incredibly rewarding. It requires a mix of creativity, strategy, and business acumen. So, if you're a product designer with big dreams, don't be afraid to take the leap and start bringing your ideas to life. With the right approach and a bit of luck, you just might create the next big thing!

Intellectual property and patents

This is the legal side of product design. It may not be the most exciting topic, but it's an important one nonetheless. Intellectual property refers to the legal rights that protect creations of the mind, such as inventions, designs, and artistic works. And patents are a form of intellectual property that protect inventions and new ideas. Now, why is this important for product designers? Well, as a product designer, your creations are your bread and butter. You want to ensure that your ideas are protected from copycats and imitators, so that you can reap the rewards of your hard work. That's where patents come in.

Getting a patent can be a lengthy and expensive process, but it's often worth it in the long run. It gives you exclusive rights to your invention for a set period of time, and allows you to prevent others from making, using, or selling your invention without your permission.

But not all products are eligible for patents, and not all product designers choose to go down that route. There are other forms of intellectual property protection, such as trademarks and copyrights, that may be more suitable for your particular situation. One thing to keep in mind is that intellectual property laws can vary by country, so it's important to do your research and ensure that your creations are protected wherever you plan to market them. It's also a good idea to work with a lawyer who specializes in intellectual property, to ensure that you're taking the necessary steps to protect your creations. At the end of the day, intellectual property and patents may not be the most glamorous aspects of product design, but they're crucial to ensuring that your ideas are protected and that you're able to profit from your hard work. So, if you're a product designer with big dreams, don't forget to protect your ideas and consider the legal side of your business.

Branding and marketing

Now we're getting into the fun stuff! As a product designer, your creations are your baby, and you want to make sure that they're getting the attention they deserve. That's where branding and marketing come in.

First, let's talk about branding. Your brand is more than just a logo or a name – it's the entire identity of your product. It's what sets you apart from the competition, and what resonates with your target audience. Developing a strong brand can help you build trust with customers, and create a loyal following.

So, how do you develop a strong brand? It starts with understanding your target audience and what they value. You want to create a brand that speaks to their needs and desires, and that reflects the personality of your product. This could involve creating a unique logo, developing a color palette, and crafting a brand voice that resonates with your audience.

Once you have a strong brand identity, it's time to start thinking about marketing. Marketing is all about getting your product in front of the right people, and convincing them to give it a try. There are a variety of marketing tactics you can use, from social media ads to influencer partnerships to email campaigns.

One key aspect of marketing is storytelling. People don't just buy products – they buy the stories and emotions behind them. You want to create a narrative around your product that resonates with your target audience and helps them understand why your product is unique and valuable.

Another important aspect of marketing is customer engagement. You want to create a dialogue with your customers and foster a sense of community around your product. This could involve hosting events, creating online forums or Facebook groups, or responding to customer inquiries and feedback. Here are some steps to help you with branding and marketing your product:

- **Step 1:** Define your target audience Before you can start building your brand and marketing your product, you need to know who your target audience is. Ask yourself questions like: Who is my ideal customer? What are their pain points? What do they value? The more you know about your target audience, the easier it will be to create a brand that resonates with them.

- **Step 2:** Develop your brand identity Once you've defined your target audience, it's time to start developing your brand identity. This could involve creating a unique logo, selecting a color palette, and developing a brand voice that resonates with your target audience.

- **Step 3:** Craft your brand narrative Your brand narrative is the story behind your product – it's what sets you apart from the competition and creates an emotional connection with your customers. Think about what makes your product unique and valuable, and how you can communicate that to your target audience.

- **Step 4:** Choose your marketing tactics There are countless marketing tactics you can use to promote your product, from social media ads to email campaigns to influencer partnerships. Think about what tactics will be most effective for reaching your target audience, and how you can create a cohesive marketing strategy that speaks to your brand narrative.

- **Step 5:** Engage with your audience Marketing isn't just about promoting your product – it's also about engaging with your audience and creating a sense of community around your brand. Respond to customer feedback and inquiries, create opportunities for customer engagement (such as events or online forums), and foster a sense of loyalty and connection with your customers.

- **Step 6:** Measure your success Finally, it's important to measure the success of your branding and marketing efforts.

Use tools like Google Analytics or social media metrics to track the effectiveness of your marketing campaigns, and adjust your strategy accordingly.

Ultimately, branding and marketing are all about creating a strong, lasting relationship between your product and your customers. It takes time and effort to build a successful brand, but the rewards are worth it. So, if you're a product designer with big dreams, don't forget to put some thought into your branding and marketing strategy. With the right approach, you can create a product that truly resonates with your target audience and stands out from the crowd.

Launching and scaling products

This is one of the most exciting (and challenging) parts of product design! Here are some tips for getting your product out there and growing your business:

- **Step 1:** Plan your launch strategy Before you can launch your product, you need to have a solid plan in place. This might include things like identifying your target audience, setting a launch date, creating a marketing campaign, and preparing your website and social media channels for the launch.

- **Step 2:** Generate buzz and excitement In the weeks leading up to your launch, it's important to generate buzz and excitement around your product. Consider hosting a pre-launch event or offering exclusive discounts to early adopters. Reach out to influencers or journalists in your industry and invite them to review your product or write about your launch.

- **Step 3:** Launch with a bang When launch day arrives, make sure you're ready to go all out. Create a launch announcement video, host a live stream event, and blast your social media channels with announcements and promotions. This is your chance to make a big splash and get your product in front of as many people as possible.

- **Step 4:** Listen to feedback and iterate Once your product is out in the world, it's important to listen to feedback and make any necessary improvements.

Take customer feedback seriously, and be open to iterating on your product to make it even better.

- **Step 5:** Scale your business As your product gains traction, it's important to think about how you can scale your business to keep up with demand. This might involve hiring additional team members, expanding your manufacturing capabilities, or investing in new marketing channels.

- **Step 6:** Build customer loyalty Finally, as your business grows, it's important to focus on building customer loyalty. Offer exceptional customer service, create a sense of community around your brand, and consistently deliver high-quality products. This will help you retain customers and build a strong, loyal fanbase.

Remember, launching and scaling a product takes time, effort, and a lot of hard work. But by staying focused, listening to feedback, and continuously improving, you can build a successful business and bring your product to the masses. Good luck!

Case studies of successful product launches

There are so many examples of case studies of companies that launched their products successfully and have scaled since there first launch. Here are a few examples that might inspire you as you work on your own product launch:

- **Apple iPhone**
  When Apple launched the first iPhone in 2007, it was a game-changer in the world of mobile phones. Apple focused on creating a product that was intuitive and easy to use, and the company's marketing strategy emphasized the phone's simplicity and sleek design. The iPhone quickly became a must-have item, and Apple's innovative product design helped the company establish itself as a leader in the tech industry.

- **Peloton Bike**
  When Peloton launched its interactive exercise bike in 2014, it quickly gained a following among fitness enthusiasts who loved the convenience of being able to take live or on-demand classes from home. Peloton's marketing strategy

focused on building a sense of community around the product, and the company's emphasis on high-quality design and technology helped it stand out in a crowded market. Today, Peloton is valued at over $30 billion.

- **Tesla Model S**
  When Tesla launched the Model S in 2012, it was a game-changer in the world of electric vehicles. Tesla focused on creating a car that was not only environmentally friendly, but also luxurious and high-performance. The company's emphasis on sleek design, advanced technology, and exceptional customer service helped it build a loyal fanbase, and today Tesla is one of the most valuable car companies in the world.

- **Airbnb**
  When Airbnb launched in 2008, it was a disruptive new player in the world of hospitality. The company's innovative platform allowed people to rent out their homes or apartments to travelers, and its emphasis on creating a unique and personalized experience helped it

stand out in a crowded market. Airbnb's marketing strategy focused on building trust and community among its users, and today the company is valued at over $100 billion.

- **Nest Thermostat**
  When Nest launched its smart thermostat in 2011, it quickly became a hit with consumers who were looking for ways to save energy and reduce their environmental impact. The company's focus on sleek design and intuitive technology helped it stand out in a crowded market, and its marketing strategy emphasized the product's ability to learn and adapt to users' behavior. Nest was acquired by Google in 2014 for $3.2 billion.

- **GoPro**
  When GoPro launched its first action camera in 2004, it was a niche product aimed primarily at extreme sports enthusiasts. However, the company's emphasis on high-quality design, durability, and ease of use helped it gain a loyal following among a wider audience. GoPro's marketing strategy

focused on creating compelling user-generated content that showcased the product's capabilities, and the company went public in 2014 with a valuation of over $3 billion.

- **Fitbit**
When Fitbit launched its first activity tracker in 2009, it was a pioneer in the wearable technology market. The company's focus on creating a product that was easy to use, reliable, and affordable helped it gain a wide audience, and its marketing strategy emphasized the product's ability to help users track their fitness goals and improve their overall health. Fitbit went public in 2015 with a valuation of over $4 billion.

- **Warby Parker**
When Warby Parker launched its online eyewear company in 2010, it disrupted the traditional brick-and-mortar retail model and made affordable, stylish eyewear accessible to a wider audience. The company's emphasis on high-quality design, personalized customer service, and social responsibility helped it gain a

loyal following, and its marketing strategy focused on creating a sense of community around the brand. Today, Warby Parker is valued at over $3 billion.

These are just a few examples of successful product launches that have transformed industries and established new standards for product design and marketing. Each of these companies took risks, embraced innovation, and focused on creating a product that truly resonated with its target audience. By taking inspiration from these success stories, you can create a product launch that is equally impactful and memorable.

Chapter 9: Product Design for Different Industries

Are you ready to dive into the fascinating world of product design across different industries? From consumer electronics to medical devices to automotive, product design is a crucial element in creating successful products that meet the needs of consumers and businesses alike. Each industry has its own unique challenges and considerations when it comes to product design, from regulatory requirements to user experience to materials and manufacturing processes. But no matter the industry, the goal of product design remains the same: to create products that are functional, aesthetically pleasing, and meet the needs of the target market. So grab a cup of coffee and let's explore the exciting world of product design for different industries!

Product design in tech

Product design in the tech industry has exploded in popularity in recent years. With the rise of smartphones, tablets, and wearable devices, designers are constantly pushing the limits of what is possible with technology. In this chapter, we'll explore the world of product design in tech, including the challenges, trends, and exciting opportunities that come with this field.

First and foremost, one of the biggest challenges of product design in tech is keeping up with rapidly evolving technology. Designers must stay up to date on the latest advancements in hardware, software, and user interface design to create products that are relevant, functional, and visually appealing. This can be a daunting task, but it's also what makes this field so exciting. Another important consideration in tech product design is user experience (UX) design. With so many devices and applications on the market, designers must focus on creating products that are intuitive, easy to use, and provide a seamless experience for users. This involves extensive user research and testing, as well as a deep understanding of human behavior and psychology.

One of the most exciting trends in tech product design is the move towards more personalized, adaptive products. With the help of artificial intelligence and machine learning, designers are now able to create products that can learn and adapt to individual users over time. This allows for a more customized and personalized experience, and can greatly enhance the overall user experience.

In terms of specific tools and software used in tech product design, there are many options available. Sketch and Figma are two popular design tools used for creating wireframes, mockups, and user interfaces. Adobe Creative Suite is also commonly used for graphic design and visual content creation. For prototyping, designers often turn to tools like InVision, Marvel, or Proto.io.

Overall, product design in tech is a fascinating and constantly evolving field that requires creativity, technical expertise, and a deep understanding of user needs and behavior. While it can be challenging to keep up with the latest advancements, it's also incredibly rewarding to create products that can change the way people interact with technology.

Product design in tech is an exciting and constantly evolving field. With new technologies and innovations emerging all the time, there is always something new to explore and discover. In this field, there are several key features that designers need to consider when creating products. Let's take a closer look:

- **User Experience (UX):** User experience refers to how a user interacts with a product, and how the product makes the user feel. UX design is focused on creating products that are easy and intuitive to use, and that provide a positive experience for the user.

- **User Interface (UI):** User interface design is the process of designing the visual elements of a product, such as buttons, menus, and icons. The goal of UI design is to make the product visually appealing and easy to use.

- **Interaction Design:** Interaction design is concerned with the way users interact with a product. This includes things like how users navigate through a product, how they perform actions, and how the product responds to their inputs.

- **Industrial Design:** Industrial design is the process of designing the physical form of a product. This includes things like the shape, size, and materials used in the product.

- **Design Thinking:** Design thinking is a problem-solving approach that is focused on understanding the needs of users and creating solutions that meet those needs. It involves empathy, creativity, and experimentation to develop innovative solutions to complex problems.

- **Rapid Prototyping:** Rapid prototyping is the process of creating quick, low-cost versions of a product in order to test and refine the design. This can be done using 3D printing, laser cutting, or other techniques.

- **Design for Manufacturability:** Design for manufacturability (DFM) is the process of designing products in a way that makes them easy and cost-effective to manufacture. This involves considering factors like materials, manufacturing processes, and assembly methods.

In conclusion, product design in tech is a multifaceted field that requires a wide range of skills and knowledge. From user experience and interface design to industrial design and rapid prototyping, there are many different features that designers need to consider when creating products that are both functional and visually appealing. By combining creativity, empathy, and technical skills, designers can create products that meet the needs of users while pushing the boundaries of what is possible.

Product design in tech requires a range of tools and software to create high-quality designs. Here are some of the most common tools used in product design in tech and their functions:

- **Sketch:** Sketch is a vector graphics editor that is used for UI and UX design. It is primarily used for designing mobile apps, websites, and other digital products.

- **Adobe Creative Suite:** The Adobe Creative Suite is a collection of software applications that includes Photoshop,

Illustrator, and InDesign. Each of these applications has its own specific use in product design.

- **Figma:** Figma is a collaborative design tool used for creating digital interfaces. It allows multiple designers to work on the same project at the same time, making it a popular choice for larger design teams.

- **InVision:** InVision is a prototyping tool that allows designers to create interactive mockups of their designs. It also has a range of other features, including design collaboration and workflow management.

- **Procreate:** Procreate is a digital painting app designed for the iPad. It is primarily used for creating digital art and illustrations.

- **SolidWorks:** SolidWorks is a 3D CAD software used for mechanical design. It is popular among engineers and designers working on products with complex mechanical components.

- **AutoCAD:** AutoCAD is a software used for creating 2D and 3D designs. It is primarily used for architecture, engineering, and construction.

- **Blender:** Blender is a 3D modeling and animation software used for creating 3D designs and animations. It is a popular choice for product designers working on complex 3D models.

- **Tinkercad:** Tinkercad is a free, browser-based CAD software designed for beginners. It is often used in educational settings to teach students the basics of 3D design.

- **Rhinoceros 3D:** Rhinoceros 3D is a 3D modeling software used for creating complex 3D models. It is often used in product design for creating detailed 3D prototypes and renderings.

These are just a few of the many tools and software applications used in product design in tech. Depending on the specific project, designers may use a combination of these tools to create high-quality designs.

Product design in fashion and apparel

When we think of product design, we often think of tech gadgets or household appliances. But product design is an important aspect of fashion and apparel as well. From shoes to dresses, product design plays a significant role in creating stylish, functional and sustainable fashion products. In fashion, product design involves creating a concept for a product, sketching the idea, choosing materials, creating a prototype, and then finalizing the design for production. The main goal is to create clothing and accessories that are not only aesthetically pleasing but also functional, comfortable and durable.

One of the most important tools in fashion product design is the computer-aided design (CAD) software. CAD software allows designers to create digital designs of their products, which can be easily manipulated and modified. This is a huge time-saver and allows designers to experiment with different designs and materials without having to create multiple physical prototypes. Some popular CAD software used in fashion product design includes Adobe Illustrator, CorelDRAW, and CLO.

Another important tool in fashion product design is the pattern-making software. Pattern-making software helps designers create the blueprint of the product, including the shapes and sizes of the pieces that will make up the final product. This is essential in ensuring that the product fits correctly and looks aesthetically pleasing. Some popular pattern-making software includes Optitex and Gerber Technology.

In addition to software, fashion designers also use physical tools such as mannequins, sewing machines, and cutting tools. These tools help designers create physical prototypes of their designs, which can be used for testing and refinement.

Mannequins are used to create a realistic representation of the human body, which helps designers understand how the product will fit and look on an actual person. Sewing machines and cutting tools are used to create the final product, ensuring that the materials are cut and sewn correctly.

One important aspect of fashion product design is sustainability. As the fashion industry becomes more aware of its environmental impact, designers are increasingly incorporating sustainable materials and production methods into their designs. This includes using recycled fabrics, reducing waste in the production process, and creating products that are designed to last.

In conclusion, fashion product design is a vital aspect of the fashion industry, and it involves a combination of digital and physical tools. The use of CAD software, pattern-making software, mannequins, sewing machines, and cutting tools helps designers create functional and aesthetically pleasing products that are designed to fit well and last long. As the industry continues to evolve, sustainability is becoming an increasingly important consideration in fashion product design.

Product design in consumer goods

From the latest gadgets to the hottest trends, consumer goods are all around us. As such, product design in consumer goods plays a crucial role in the success of any business.

At its core, product design in consumer goods is about creating products that people will love and want to buy. It involves everything from designing the look and feel of a product, to selecting the right materials, to ensuring that the product is functional and easy to use.

To achieve these goals, designers in this field use a variety of tools and techniques. Let's take a look at some of the most common:

- **Sketching and ideation tools:** Sketching is an essential tool for product designers in consumer goods, allowing them to quickly visualize and iterate on ideas. Tools like Adobe Illustrator, Sketch, and Procreate are popular choices for creating sketches and ideation.

- **3D modeling software:** Once an initial concept has been developed, designers can create detailed 3D models of their products using software like SolidWorks, Autodesk Fusion 360, or Rhino. This allows them to refine the design and test its functionality before moving on to manufacturing.

- **Rendering software:** To create photorealistic images of their products, designers use rendering software such as KeyShot, V-Ray, or Blender. These tools allow them to create high-quality images that can be used for marketing and advertising.

- **CAD software:** Computer-aided design (CAD) software is used to create detailed technical drawings of products. These drawings are used by manufacturers to create molds and tooling for production. Popular CAD software in consumer goods include AutoCAD, Creo, and Solid Edge.

- **Product lifecycle management (PLM) software:** PLM software is used to manage the entire lifecycle of a product, from design to manufacturing to distribution. These tools help designers and manufacturers collaborate more effectively and ensure that the product is produced on time and within budget. Popular PLM software in consumer goods include Arena Solutions, Oracle Agile PLM, and PTC Windchill.

When it comes to designing consumer goods, it's important to keep in mind the end user. Designers need to create products that not only look great, but also meet the needs and expectations of the people who will use them. By using the right tools and techniques, designers can create products that are both functional and desirable, and that stand out in a crowded marketplace.

Product design in industrial and engineering fields

Industrial and engineering product design is a fascinating field that involves developing and creating new products, tools, and systems to improve efficiency and productivity in a variety of industries. From aerospace and automotive engineering to consumer electronics and heavy machinery, industrial and engineering product design plays a critical role in shaping the world we live in.

When it comes to product design in this field, the focus is on creating functional, safe, and reliable products that meet specific industry needs. Industrial and engineering product designers use a wide range of tools and techniques to bring their ideas to life, from computer-aided design (CAD) software to rapid prototyping machines.

Let's take a closer look at some of the tools and techniques used in industrial and engineering product design:

- **Computer-Aided Design (CAD) Software:** CAD software is an essential tool for industrial and engineering product designers. It allows designers to create detailed 2D and 3D digital models of products, parts, and assemblies, which can be easily manipulated, refined, and shared with others.

- **Finite Element Analysis (FEA) Software:** FEA software is used to simulate how a product will behave under various conditions and loads, allowing designers to identify potential weaknesses or areas for improvement before the product is built.

- **Rapid Prototyping Machines:** Rapid prototyping machines are used to create physical prototypes of products quickly and accurately. These machines use various materials such as plastics, metals, and composites to create physical models that can be tested and refined before production.

- **Simulation and Modeling Tools:** Simulation and modeling tools allow designers to test and optimize products before they are built. These tools simulate how products will behave under different conditions, allowing designers to make informed decisions about product design and performance.

- **Materials Testing Equipment:** Materials testing equipment is used to test the strength, durability, and other properties of materials used in product design. This information is critical in selecting the best materials for a given application.

In addition to these tools and techniques, industrial and engineering product designers also rely on a deep understanding of industry standards and regulations, as well as strong problem-solving and communication skills.

In summary, product design in industrial and engineering fields is an exciting and complex field that involves creating functional and efficient products. With a wide range of tools and techniques at their disposal, industrial and engineering product designers can bring their ideas to life and make a real impact on the world around us.

Chapter 10: Future of Product Design

The future of product design is an exciting and rapidly evolving landscape, as new technologies, materials, and consumer behaviors continue to shape the way products are designed and manufactured. Here are some potential developments and trends that may shape the future of product design:

- **Sustainability:** As concerns over climate change and resource depletion continue to grow, sustainability is likely to become an even more important consideration in product design. Designers will increasingly focus on creating products that are environmentally friendly, long-lasting, and easy to recycle or repair.

- **Personalization:** With advances in manufacturing technology such as 3D printing, it may become more common for consumers to customize products to their own preferences. This could lead to a greater focus on mass customization and the use of digital tools to create personalized products.

- **Augmented Reality:** Augmented reality (AR) technology has the potential to revolutionize the way products are designed and experienced. Designers could use AR to visualize and manipulate products in real-time, allowing for faster and more efficient design iterations.

- **Artificial Intelligence:** As AI becomes more sophisticated, it could have a significant impact on product design. AI-powered tools could help designers generate new ideas, identify design flaws, and predict consumer preferences.

- **Wearable Technology:** With the growing popularity of wearable technology, designers will need to consider how products can be integrated into a user's daily life. This may require a greater focus on ergonomics, user experience, and connectivity.

- **Biomimicry:** As designers continue to look for inspiration in nature, biomimicry may become an even more important tool in product design. By emulating the forms and functions of natural systems, designers can create products that are more efficient, sustainable, and aesthetically pleasing.

- **Collaborative Design:** With advances in communication technology, it may become easier for designers to collaborate with clients, stakeholders, and other designers from around the world. This could lead to more diverse and innovative products that reflect a wider range of perspectives and needs.

- **Virtual Reality:** Virtual reality (VR) technology has the potential to transform the way products are designed and tested. Designers could use VR to create immersive product simulations, allowing them to test designs and gather feedback before physical prototypes are created.

Tools that may play a role in shaping the future of product design include:
- 3D printing software and hardware
- CAD software

- Augmented and virtual reality tools
- Artificial intelligence and machine learning tools
- Collaborative design software
- Sustainability analysis software
- Wearable technology design tools

Overall, the future of product design looks bright, with a wide range of exciting developments and trends likely to shape the industry in the years ahead. As new technologies and materials continue to emerge, designers will need to stay flexible and adaptable, always looking for new and innovative ways to create products that meet the needs and desires of consumers while minimizing their environmental impact.

Emerging technologies and their impact on product design

Emerging technologies are rapidly transforming the way we approach product design. From artificial intelligence to 3D printing, these new technologies are offering designers and manufacturers a plethora of new tools to work with. In this article, we'll explore some of the most exciting emerging technologies and their impact on product design.

- **Artificial intelligence (AI)**
  AI is already being used in a variety of ways in product design, from creating custom product recommendations based on user data to generating complex 3D models. In the future, AI could enable designers to automatically generate design concepts, optimize designs for manufacturing, and simulate product performance. AI-powered tools could also help reduce waste and improve sustainability by optimizing material usage and reducing overproduction.

- **Virtual and augmented reality (VR/AR)**
  VR and AR are already being used by designers to create immersive product experiences and visualize products in real-world environments. In the future, VR/AR could be used to simulate product usage and testing, allowing designers to identify and address potential issues before a product is ever manufactured. These technologies could also improve collaboration between

designers and manufacturers, allowing teams to work together in a shared virtual environment.

- **3D printing**
  3D printing has already revolutionized product design by enabling designers to rapidly prototype and test their designs. In the future, 3D printing could become an even more integral part of the design process, with printers capable of producing finished products on-demand. This could enable companies to reduce waste, cut down on inventory costs, and create more customized products.

- **Internet of Things (IoT)**
  IoT devices are already being integrated into a wide range of products, from smart home appliances to wearable fitness trackers. In the future, IoT could become an even more integral part of product design, with products designed to seamlessly integrate with other devices and services. This could enable products to offer new features and functionality, as well as enable manufacturers to collect valuable data on how their products are being used.

- **Nanotechnology** Nanotechnology is still in its early stages, but it has the potential to revolutionize product design by enabling the creation of new materials and products with unprecedented properties. Nanotechnology could enable the creation of products that are stronger, lighter, and more durable than anything we've seen before.

As these technologies continue to evolve, product designers will need to adapt and learn how to use them effectively. However, the possibilities they offer are exciting, and they have the potential to transform the way we think about and approach product design.

Trends in sustainability and social responsibility

Sustainability and social responsibility are becoming increasingly important considerations in product design. As consumers become more aware of the impact their purchases have on the environment and society, there is a growing demand for products that are designed with sustainability and ethical practices in mind. In this article, we will explore some of the current trends in sustainability and social responsibility in product design.

- **Circular design:** One of the most significant trends in sustainability is circular design. The concept of a circular economy is based on the idea of keeping materials in use for as long as possible, and then recovering and regenerating them at the end of their life. In product design, this means creating products that can be easily disassembled and recycled at the end of their life cycle. This approach helps to reduce waste and preserve natural resources, and is becoming increasingly popular among companies that are committed to sustainability.

- **Sustainable materials:** Another trend in sustainability is the use of sustainable materials in product design. This includes materials that are renewable, biodegradable, and non-toxic. Examples of sustainable materials include bamboo, recycled plastic, and organic cotton. By using sustainable materials, designers can reduce the environmental impact of their products and create a more sustainable future.

- **Social responsibility:** Social responsibility is another important consideration in product design. This includes ensuring that workers involved in the production of a product are treated fairly and with respect, and that the product does not have any negative impact on society. This trend is particularly relevant in the fashion industry, where there have been increasing concerns about labor practices and environmental impact.

- **Design for disassembly:** Design for disassembly is a trend that is closely related to circular design. It involves creating products that are easy to disassemble and recycle at the end of their life cycle. This approach helps to reduce waste and makes it easier to recover valuable materials for reuse.

- **Local sourcing:** Local sourcing is a trend that involves using materials and resources that are sourced locally, rather than being shipped from overseas. This approach helps to reduce the environmental impact of shipping and transportation, and can also help to support local communities and businesses.

- **Energy efficiency:** Energy efficiency is becoming an increasingly important consideration in product design. This includes designing products that use less energy, such as LED lighting and energy-efficient appliances. By reducing energy consumption, designers can help to reduce greenhouse gas emissions and create a more sustainable future.

- **Sustainable packaging:** Sustainable packaging is another trend in sustainability that is becoming increasingly important in product design. This includes using packaging that is biodegradable or recyclable, and reducing the amount of packaging used in products. By using sustainable packaging, designers can help to reduce waste and minimize the environmental impact of their products.

In conclusion, sustainability and social responsibility are becoming increasingly important considerations in product design. By incorporating these trends into their design practices, designers can create products that are both environmentally and socially responsible. From circular design to sustainable materials, designers have a range of tools at their disposal to help create a more sustainable future.

The future of product design education and careers

The field of product design is constantly evolving and changing, and so are the educational and career opportunities in the industry. In this comprehensive article, we will discuss the future of product design education and careers, including emerging trends, new technologies, and changing job markets.

Education:

- **Interdisciplinary approach:** In the future, product design education will become more interdisciplinary. Students will be encouraged to explore and incorporate diverse fields such as sustainability, engineering, psychology, and business into their design practices.

- **Focus on digital skills:** As technology continues to advance, product design education will also place more emphasis on digital skills such as CAD (Computer-Aided Design), 3D modeling, and prototyping.

- **Virtual and augmented reality:** With the rise of virtual and augmented reality, product design programs will incorporate these technologies into their curriculums, allowing students to explore and create in a virtual environment.

- **Globalization:** With the world becoming increasingly interconnected, product design education will also become more global, providing students with opportunities to learn from and collaborate with designers from around the world.

Careers:

- **Rise of freelance and remote work:** With the increasing accessibility of digital tools and the rise of the gig economy, product designers will have more opportunities to work as freelancers or remotely.

- **Emergence of new industries:** As technology continues to advance, new industries such as robotics, smart home devices, and wearable technology will emerge, creating new opportunities for product designers.

- **Sustainability and social responsibility:** Product designers will be increasingly called upon to incorporate sustainability and social responsibility into their work, with a focus on creating products that are environmentally friendly, ethically sourced, and socially responsible.

- **Collaboration and cross-functional teams:** As product design becomes more complex and interdisciplinary, designers will need to work in collaboration with engineers, business leaders, and other stakeholders to bring products to market.

- **Emphasis on soft skills:** In addition to technical skills, product designers will need to develop strong communication, collaboration, and problem-solving skills to be successful in the industry.

Tools:

- **Virtual and augmented reality:** Virtual and augmented reality technologies will continue to play a significant role in product design, allowing designers to create and test products in a virtual environment before moving on to physical prototypes.

- **Artificial intelligence:** AI-powered design tools will become more prevalent, providing designers with the ability to automate repetitive tasks, analyze data, and generate new design concepts.

- **Sustainability assessment tools:** As sustainability becomes a more critical consideration in product design, new tools will emerge to help designers assess the environmental impact of their products.

- **Collaborative platforms:** Collaborative platforms such as Slack and Trello will continue to gain popularity, allowing designers to work more efficiently with cross-functional teams.

In conclusion, the future of product design education and careers is exciting and filled with possibilities. As the industry continues to evolve, designers will need to adapt to new technologies, industries, and social and environmental considerations. By developing interdisciplinary skills, embracing emerging technologies, and focusing on sustainability and social responsibility, product designers can shape the future of the industry and create products that are not only beautiful and functional but also make a positive impact on the world.

Conclusion

Product design learning is a crucial aspect of any designer's journey. The process of creating new products that are functional, beautiful, and sustainable is a complex one that requires a wide range of skills, knowledge, and experience. By studying product design, individuals can gain the necessary skills and knowledge to create products that are not only aesthetically pleasing but also meet the needs of consumers, the environment, and society as a whole. Additionally, product design education is constantly evolving, and it is important for designers to keep up with emerging trends, technologies, and tools. Whether pursuing a formal education or seeking out self-directed learning opportunities, product design education is a valuable investment for anyone looking to enter or advance in this exciting field.

Summary of key takeaways

It's clear that product design is a fascinating field that requires creativity, technical skills, and a deep understanding of user needs and trends. From designing products for manufacturing and sustainability, to using emerging technologies and software, product design is a constantly evolving field with plenty of opportunities for innovation. Here are the key takeaways from the topics covered in this book:

- Product design is a multi-disciplinary field that involves creative problem-solving, empathy, and a deep understanding of user needs and wants.
- The design process involves ideation, prototyping, testing, and iteration to create products that are functional, aesthetically pleasing, and sustainable.
- Designers need to consider various factors such as materials, manufacturing processes, assembly and disassembly, and end-of-life disposal to reduce environmental impact and promote sustainability.
- The use of design tools and software has revolutionized product design in various industries, including tech, fashion, consumer goods, and industrial engineering.
- Emerging technologies such as AI, 3D printing, and VR/AR are transforming the product design landscape and enabling designers to create more innovative and personalized products.

- Trends in sustainability and social responsibility are driving the demand for more environmentally friendly and ethically produced products.
- The future of product design education and careers is evolving to include more interdisciplinary training, a focus on emerging technologies, and a commitment to sustainability and social responsibility.

Overall, product design is an exciting and dynamic field that requires a unique blend of creativity, technical skills, and a deep understanding of user needs and the impact of design on society and the environment. Aspiring product designers should focus on honing their skills in areas such as sketching, 3D modeling, prototyping, and user research. It's also important to keep up with the latest tools and technologies, as well as emerging trends in sustainability and social responsibility.

Product design education is another key consideration, with a range of options available from traditional universities to online courses and bootcamps. And for those already in the field, there are plenty of opportunities for career growth and specialization, with roles ranging from industrial designer to UX designer and beyond.

Product design is a field that offers endless possibilities for those with a passion for creativity, problem-solving, and innovation. So whether you're just starting out or looking to take your career to the next level, there's never been a better time to dive into the exciting world of product design!

Final thoughts on the importance of product design

Product design is an essential aspect of our lives, and it affects everything we interact with. From the smartphone in our hands to the chair we sit on, product design influences our daily experiences. It's a powerful tool that can improve functionality, aesthetics, and even our well-being.

As we've seen throughout this book, product design involves a range of skills, tools, and considerations. It's a multifaceted discipline that requires creativity, technical knowledge, and empathy for the user. Moreover, product design has a significant impact on the environment, social responsibility, and sustainability. It's crucial that we consider the life-cycle of the products we design, the materials we use, and the impact on society and the planet. In conclusion, product design is an exciting and important field that has the potential to make a positive impact on the world. It's a constantly evolving discipline that demands adaptability, innovation, and a deep understanding of human needs and desires. As technology advances and new challenges arise, product designers will continue to play a crucial role in shaping the future.

Now that you've learned about the many facets of product design and its impact on our world, it's time to take action. Whether you're a professional designer, a student, or simply interested in the field, there are plenty of ways to apply what you've learned. Consider taking a course or workshop to hone your skills, exploring new design tools and technologies, or seeking out sustainable and socially responsible design opportunities. You can also support companies and brands that prioritize product design and innovation. Remember, product design is more than just aesthetics and functionality; it has the power to shape our world and influence the way we live our lives. So, let's embrace the potential of product design and use it to create a better future for us all.